Ere –Voice

Books by Carl Rakosi

Amulet
Ere-Voice

Ere-Voice

by Carl Rakosi

New Directions

ACKNOWLEDGMENTS
Some of these poems first appeared in the following magazines and books: *Albatross, The American Literary Anthology 3, Caterpillar, Chelsea, Grosseteste Review, Inside Outer Space* (anthology), *The Iowa Review, Midstream, The Minnesota Review, The Nation, New Directions 23, The Park, Quarterly Review of Literature, Stony Brook, Sumac.*

I owe much to Yaddo, where most of these poems were written.
I wish there were a catwalk from them to my dear family and friends.
C.R.

First published clothbound and as ND Paperbook 321 in 1971
Published simultaneously in Canada by McClelland & Stewart, Ltd.
Manufactured in the United States of America

New Directions Books are published for James Laughlin
by New Directions Publishing Corporation,
333 Sixth Avenue, New York 10014

Ere–Voice

"Who is there

        to attain What?"

the master of Ch'an

        the medium of the ocean

A Tablet Against Aging

You are as fixed in me,
                    o loyal wife,
as the bright
                point of Canopus
to the helmsman.

Evening with My Granddaughters

o for a world with a string and a kitten
and Tipsy who loves us so much
                                    he pees

and you and I.

In a Warm Bath

Buddha is not more strange
                              and impersonal
than you, o belly
                    waiting for the doctor's probe,
or you, phallus
                  wrinkled as an old crocodile
in a salt marsh. Horn of schlemiel!
Uxorious! Imperative! Boaster! Father!
Outside the order of imagination
                              and the public interest.

Father! In what way father? Too old. Can't tell him though.
Nor he me. Too much pain in the eyes.
His black obsidian gaze is closed to me.
May be just light refracted.
                              Why closed?
He can be fond and amiable. Dangerous to press for more.

Engage in argument. God help me!
Like an owl zeroing in on a mouse
aware too late of its exposure
he breaks from ambush with transfixing logic.

Yet he is sympathetic. The clarity I taught him
he has turned against me, and I am satisfied.
I say a man has integrity. For this he cares.
And I. Looks at me long and deep,
a straight beam unavoidable. And I to him.
I was made father for this.
Eyes clasped,
               down we go into a mine
without a guide or map, and damn the pinched face
of the Puritan who holds us back.
Be careful though in table talk.
Hold in the thought, When I am gone,
though all I mean is fact faceless.
Can't bear to see him laid low.
Careful not to give him pain,
I swear it as a father,
until the time when he and I
must put the figurative prayer shawl
on together and join Abraham.

Inventor of the wheel,
               save us from cancer!

Bless this water.
               I must bathe more often.

Leah

Belial my oaf warned me
she would not be
                    suitable for a poem—
bedded and tongued together
                            too long.

She does not belong
                    to my ulcerous subliminal.
She is natural.
She runs off like rain water.
I could not put her
                    under the hard master
of an image
            for my own need.

So since poetry is more abstract,
                            more for its registrar,
give me her smile
                    and let us hug and romp
in the plain life

or I am lost!

The Elder Sister

When she was four
a sister cooed
and took her mother.

What is mine?
was then her question.
End of innocence.

She knew now
she was envious
and overbearing.

God, how she wept
and hated then,
yet looked at me

as if to ask,
Why are you
sad?

Come into my room.
I'll hide my pain
and we'll play.

Four * Part Invention for the Organ

Origin gapes
            and would speak.
Speak!
            Are you tormented?
I hear the stone of sound.
Deus in reeds.
            Titans sob.
From the mouth of Okeanus
to the orifice of chaos
it verberates and roams,
its destiny never
to enter matter.
Hence its pitch is off.
Not bad for souls.
So beautiful is matter,
souls are purified
and punished there.

Old cloud chamber.
Origen cut his balls
            off there.

All dead,
   old theologies.
No more listeners.
Old dead.
Still it speaks.
Neither sorrow nor the absence of it,
only apprehension
which freezes souls
and hangs them from a beam
where they can only bound
on air currents.

Again it speaks
as from a crater
dry and angry,
breath of dogma.
Quake, limbs!
Open, bowels!
Logos is
Gnosis is
Origen is

Note: Origen is believed to have castrated himself in order to be
free of sexual impulses so that he could teach women the principles
of Christianity.

Abstractions on a Child

Sixteenth Century

A fairy magnitude
               of the order of nul

a distillation
            no bigger than a teardrop.

I am not trying
             to pass these lines off as my own.
They just flew out
            of my memory.
I thought them worth keeping
so I pinned them through
               the title for all to look at
in theoretical time
            like a butterfly,
specimen identified.

Shall I be honest with you ?
I had intended to write
             about my granddaughters
but this was as close as I could come.

The Drinking Vessel

Strange that this glass cup
                    shaped like a trumpet
is of more interest
              than the unknown Saxon
with whom it was buried.

To My Granddaughters' House

There is a hegemony
                    of mother
where the cucumber is real
but between my house
                    and yours
null turns into Titania
and a star
          is not literal.

The Old Man's Hornpipe

This puppy jumping up
to reach the mouth
        of man

this running of little girls
            like sandpipers
to get there before their thoughts do

this whippoorwill at the tail end of winter

ah, Atlantis!

Two Variations on a Theme

I

What's his offense?

He's young
and lies with women
                    in his imagination.
The apprehension of death
grips him by the neck.
He'll go as close to an old man
as to a blubber washed up
                    on the beach.

II

What's his offense?

He will not look.
The face is too old.
He will not look.

Conversation in a Hotel Room

When my time comes, I want to be out as usual
                              on the playing field
with George and Homer, not in a hotel room
                    like the Chairman of the Conference.
I'd like it to be Sunday morning. The sun is shining.
On the ground beside me are my three favorite balls.
I pick one up and hold it for a moment
and look out over the bowling green
and as I get the bead and reach back to throw
I want to just buckle under nice and easy
                              and stay down!
This is a shepherd's song
a moment as authentic
as the State Flower of Iowa
when man with offices in eighteen cities but few words
reaches for the Old Crow
and discovers Tom Sawyer in The Financial World
(I had forgotten how much I miss Tom)
and I hear a shepherd singing:
How Endearing and Inscrutable is Man.

I

From Man,
o worm,
you will extrude
the antiworm!

II

A toast to man:
as god as his word
                    at the head of his table,
grinning like a rat-trap,
                         a man of slime,
long life to him!
from the black humor
                    boys.

III

So much depends
upon

the
instant

wrist
watch

on the
executive,

a thyroid
pill,

a clean
bowel.

IV

When you've been
                  through the sabre-jet
marine pilot's
          school of nerves
and an idea
        is as real
as a horse,
you're ready for the competition.

V

"We're holding
a place for you
in The Golden Age Club."

At the sweet voice
of the program director
the retired poet jumped
as if he'd heard
a rattlesnake behind him.

VI

The day is long.
The girl technicians chat
                    and laugh about their dates
as if there were no unknown
                         pensioner on the X-ray table.

The stud days are over.
In the morning you will see
                    only aged widows
at the cashier's window
                with pachydermal patience
waiting to pay an electric bill.

The money-making days are gone.
The day is long
              in the bird sanctuary
and the periodical room.

I too therefore like the office.
We can kid each other there against
                      the long day
                      of ecology.

The Night Bus

Great Wheels.
             Better step back.
Like standing next to a pyramid.

Scale.
      Not much used
yet mighty.
            "On the scale of my life,"
a thought,
          as if I had heard
a voice.
        Instantly
the elements slip into place:
my house, the rocks, the ocean.
Is this their night orbit?
This is not where they were.

Country road
            under the headlights
speeding, beautiful,
glances off my cheek,
an abstract plane.

Burr. The tires,
as from a Scot glottis.
Gurgling then
              but soft and long,
unrolling,
          rubber slapping softly
against the cement,
the driver's foot asleep.

Dark bus body.
                    Night, the *ursprache*.
Gold out of quiet
                    light around him.
No, it is more delicate
more like an emanation
                    a man
alone
        longing.
Of my eyes
            yet outside,
a cousin to the strange,
the lovely Elizabethan line,
"We have the receipt of fern-seed,
we walk invisible."

But voices intervene:
"I get antsy. I have to stretch my legs.
Get out into a trout stream."

Deeply comforting, the ordinary,
but I contract into a cricket's pulse
and have to travel through my medium
on a higher frequency.

Night.
        Where am I?
In a dense Bartokian wood
sans entropy,
tactile with frogs;
conceivably a negative of space,
yet starts felicity.
Here am I absolutely tuned.
Call Titania to my side
for Leah can not follow me here.

Here sometimes there is no way in
except by some other poet's bungling.
Then I cry out,
                        "Not that way, this way!"
and I find myself in the wood again
and all is well.

Then an old voice
                        as from a balcony,
a lady
            sweet:
"Mother always impressed on us
that never was a long time,"
referring to her own rebelliousness
and she ought at least to try.
The way of the world:
the old are wise,
the young think they know.
This is her magic wood.
I must not mock it.

Then another:
"I gotta go back
and look under a leaf
like when I was a kid to see
if I'm really a sensitive loner
or just an image."
Intellectual.
                        Laughs.
I refuse to look pleased
or contend with his intellect.
All I want is to reach out
and touch his hand.

Who is that staring at me?
Cold eye of a pragmatist,
                    my ancient enemy.

Well, if a dog in time
can look like its master,
why not the eyes of a pragmatist,
from always fixing on a practical object,
come to look that hard?

But lutes hang in the air
                    unplayed.
The poet plots an axis
                    in space
and Leah becomes my polestar.

Poem

The ants came
to investigate
the dead
bull snake,
nibbled
at the viscera
and hurried off
with full mouths,
waving wild
antennae.

Moths alighted.
Beetles swarmed.
Flies buzzed
in the stomach.

Three crows
tugged and tore
and flew off
to their oak tree
with the skin.

In every house
men, women and children
were chewing beef.

Who was it said
"The wonder of the world
is its comprehensibility"?

"In Thy Sleep / Little Sorrows Sit and Weep"

In the night
a little crow
whose wing was broken
lay on the ground
and cried out.

Strigidae
the owl
protector of grain
heard
and glided
        soundless
nearby to a low branch.

Straight ahead he looked,
like a man,
        engraved
as on an ancient
        measuring cup,
or seated at the knee
of Michelangelo's *Night*,
waiting,
        motionless,
erect.
Not two weeks old,
the crow slept.

An hour passed.
A feather stirred.

Instantly the great
head swiveled
and the bird of prey
                                leaped,
spearing,
and carried off the body
to a distant tree stump.

Again he waited,
                        listening.

The implacable beak
then grasped it by the head
and gulped it down.
Three times he swallowed,
spitting out
                        the crow bones,
fur, and feathers.

Then the great bird,
silent on Egyptian tombs,
blinked,
                preened,
and hooted.

No One Talks About This

They go in different ways.
One hog is stationed at the far end
of the pen to decoy the others,
the hammer knocks the cow
                              to his knees,
the sheep goes gentle
                         and unsuspecting.
Then the chain is locked
around the hind leg
and the floor descends
                         from under them.
Head down they hang.
The great drum turns
the helpless objects
and conveys them slowly
to the butcher waiting
at his station
for their jugular.

The sheep is stabbed
behind the ear.

Gentle sheep, I am powerless
to mitigate your sorrow.
Men no longer weep
                      by the rivers of Babylon,
but I will speak for you.
If I forget you, may my eyes
lose their Jerusalem.

A Lamentation

After Solomon Ibn Gabirol

Awake.
Your youth is passing like smoke.
In the morning you are vital,
                              a lily swaying,
but before the evening is over,
you will be nothing but dead grass.

Why struggle over who in your family
may have come from Abraham?
It's a waste of breath.
Whether you feed on herbs
                          or Bashan rams
you, wretched man,
are already on your way into the earth.

30

Meditation

After Jehudah Halevi

How long will you remain a boy?
Dawns must end.
Behold the angels of old age.

Shake off temporal things then
the way a bird shakes off the night dew.
Dart like a swallow
                  from the raging ocean
of daily events
and pursue the Lord
in the intimate company
of souls flowing
            into His virtue.

Meditation

After Moses Ibn Ezra

Men are children of this world,
yet God has set eternity in my heart.

All my life I have been in the desert
but the world is a fresh stream.

I drink from it. How potent this water is!
How deeply I crave it!

An ocean rushes into my throat
but my thirst remains unquenched.

Meditation

After Solomon Ibn Gabirol

Three things remind me of You,
the heavens
        who are a witness to Your name
the earth
       which expands my thought
       and is the thing on which I stand
and the musing of my heart
        when I look within.

The Code

I had to pull the little maple tree
close to the house.
                    It had leaves already.
And I saw a doe standing
                    in its romaunt
munching peacefully
                    while the wolf stalked.
Such is my confusion.

When I broke it,
only the moloch unthink
                    groaned.

The seed knew
            before Sinai
it would be a root
            but not the nature
of man.

It was coded
            to become a shade tree
sized for the Colossus
                    Rameses the Second
and entered the earth
                    zigzagging
after the radish and the worm.
Its necessity would have cracked my cement
and pierced a water main.
Yet it was coded
            in the presence of the sun
to turn our breath and water
                    into deer food
and connect us to our nature
and give us peace from pursuance.

In our deadly assignation
I was coded to be contemplative
with a twig:
        out of the ground
only an hour,
        yet so downcast.
Poor Yorick!

In the root I saw a miniature
        crab apple tree
twisting into Dada.
        Insane ending.

Must all lead back to the thinker?
        Is there no
germination in a cube
        or sprouting in a sphere?

Rock Bass at Yaddo

From the hammer blow
                    of the great pump
I came to this lake,
                ripples running
as a multitude at me
                    transverse and small,
and underneath,
                the gliding over moss.

Sitting, over it, a boulder,
knuckled bulk
                mottled and piled up,
transfixed in space,
                    a coma,
sculpture its nymph.

This I saw
            before I knew I was looking.

Then a splash.
Is it possible a fish can leap
                        clear out of water,
flashing,
        mouth open,
and stay in the air,
then backflop
and disappear softly with a dragonfly?
Then two, three, further down.
I stayed.

The middle distance held me.
There hygeia was,
                    of perspective,
and could not be without shade;
and light
            weightless
as the gentle powder
                    before it has materialized,
yet clear, the cutting
                    edge of a diamond.

But the little yellow-bellied birds
were not here,
                    chirring.
They have their own mythos
                    in the pine woods.

Hush persisted, heavy
                    as of a poem
about to come into the imagination,
but nothing came.
"A pleasant stream
                    irregular in shape
with wooded banks,"
                    but why so pleasant?

Ité!
    I heard
or did I call?

This is a small stream.
It must be one
                of those minor deities
or nymphs, one of many
able to charm stones and wild beasts
and to enter the red berries
                of the *honysocle*.

Shapely she was,
transcendent as the conception of her
in the high intensity of that voice,
the italics and the exclamation mark,
and the listener shivered.

This was the signature of an older poet,
that voice in him, forgotten,
                origin forgotten,
to call out into a myth
to be with a nymph,
just the two of them in that medium,
                both timeless,
calling to her as if she were real
and he *had* to call,
no longer alive in the ordinary sense,
a strain of myth himself now,
and all because of a few jumping fish.

The poem never got written.
I had nothing myself to say.

VI   Old Hickory

When a man tells me,
                    "Elevate
them guns a little lower,"
                    I'll buy that!

VII

The indomitable Yankee
                            cactus,
Calvin Coolidge,
                used to be afraid
his most careful
              nothings
would be misconstrued.
His lips were sealed tighter
           than an old
man's scrotum
backing up from winter
           water.
When he looked the nation
straight in the eye,
nobody but nobody
                  had any question
that if cornered,
            he would not hesitate
to retreat
even from his own spittin' image.

VIII

Everybody wants to get into the act,
said Jimmie Durante,
                    even Athenagoras,
the Patriarch of Constantinople.
Three times he exchanged
the kiss of peace
                    with Paul the Sixth
and vowed in Greek
                    and Latin
before the assembled bishops
cardinals and metropolitans
                    on TV
to end their differences
and honor the seat in Rome.

Thousands of children,
                    said the press,
waved white carnations.

That did it!
          said the old maestro.
Everybody has to be a poet!

IX

Your correspondent must be kidding when he says
that OK came to us from Obediah Kelly, a freight agent
who used to sign his initials on bills of lading.

Why, there are a dozen explanations more intriguing,
such as, an invention of the early telegraphers;

or, variant of **okeh,** a Choctaw word meaning "IT IS SO"
(which may account
                    for Mrs. Nicholas Murray Butler's *horror*
at finding it in English drawing rooms by 1935
and, worse still, in The Oxford Dictionary);

or, a corruption of the harvest word, **hoacky,**
the last load brought in from the fields;

or, the identification letters for the outer keel
which used to be laid first by the early shipbuilders.

At one time it was even used as an incantation
against fleas,
                    which may explain why some people thought
it had its origin in a sign: THE PEOPLE IS OLL KORRECT

painted by Thomas Daniels, a local handyman,
on a farm wagon drawn by twenty-four horses
carrying thirty-six young women dressed in white
to a Whig rally in a grove in Champaign County, Ohio.

Another possibility is that OK stood
for Old Kinderhook, the birthplace of Martin Van Buren,
known to his supporters as The Sage of Kinderhook
and to his enemies as The Kinderhook Fox

but after five hundred of his loyal rowdies
using OK as a rallying cry were thrown out
                                        of a Whig meeting,
the *Daily Express* suggested that the word was Arabic
which read backwards meant Kicked Out.

The possibility I like best, however, is that OK stood
for Aux Quais where the French sailors
used to date American girls during the Revolutionary War.

At any rate, OK is the first word
                        learned by immigrants
and makes them instant
                democrats.

X   Folk Song

He has offices
in eighteen
cities

and still acts
like a simple
man

sitting
with cronies
in a country

store,
his legs up
on the stove

an open bottle
and all the time
in the world.

XI Strictly Iowa

They were married so long
                they were worn down
to the same element:
            two factual blue eyes
and an open freckled face
neither liberal nor conservative,
like the Revolutionary farmer,
and as sparing with an adjective
            as a short-haired dog.

XII   1924

They learned first how to handle a rifle
and went into the woods
for squirrel and pheasant
and hooked bait
with the care of a paleontologist.

At night they sat with whisky
and said to a companion
                    "Let's get drunk"
and the answer came back
                    "All right."

When they went to war and were afraid
and got shot up
and found a girl and had a family

or shot lion and climbed Kilimanjaro
and pursued the dark Iberian
                    gored
who sighted with his sword
the place of death
                    behind the bull's neck
and went in over the horns,
holding back nothing,
all they had to say was
                    "It's good
when the fall rains come"
and the answer was
                    "Swell."

Will there be no more larks
                    or Cézanne apples?

Adieu then.

XIII

Captain Patterson, the folks back home
would like to know how you feel
about your first kill.

We had just completed our mission
and were rolling out when we saw four MIG 17s
off our left wing.
        They were headed toward us
so we jettisoned our tanks
           and blew our afterburners
and climbed left.
        The lead MIG started firing.
The fight was on.
        I put our Phantom into a 70° dive.
One MIG crossed our canopy from right to left,
leaving the area at a good speed.
I was about to take off after him
When another MIG appeared at 10 o'clock high.
"That's our baby,"
        I called to Doug.
"Let's get him on the radar."
           He locked in
and for three miles we were in trail.
Then we closed in and fired the sidewinder
real smooth off our left wing.
For a long while it just trailed the MIG,
then delicately at about a thousand feet behind
it straightened out and sailed into his tailpipe.
Blew him into a brilliant fire ball.

It was a piece of cake.
        We wish they'd come up
and say hello more often.

XIV   A Mustache Drawn on Americana XIII

I'll bet you dollars to doughnuts
the Vincents hit us tonight.
The village chief just took off,
claiming he had business in Danang.

I'd like to take off myself,
all the way to Flint, Michigan.
For openers I'd show up at the airport
with a big sign, GET THE MARINES OUT OF VIETNAM.
Under that in smaller letters:
                      starting with me.

XV   Simplicity

o rare circle,
you are not in favor now.
Not much is written about you.
Perhaps not much is known about you.
But when I hear this,

"I am just a widow woman.
What do I know?"

and when I see the father of many children
hurrying to the polls in Saigon
to pick the candidate whose symbol is the plow

and when I hear an eighteen year old tell the judge
"So here is Tom Rodd.
                    I wanted to go to Selma
and Montgomery but I didn't.
I wanted to go to Washington and confront the President
                    but I didn't.
But this war is too much for me to say I didn't.
So I'm prepared to go to jail.
                    I have no beef against this court.
I want my friends to know that I'm an optimist.
I drink beer and I play the banjo."

O rare simplicity,
                    when I hear this,
I know I am in your honest presence.

XVI   1968

The atmosphere might be described
as barbed wire and cement roadblocks.

An American Embassy:
man showing
          pass
man adjusting
          camera
man filling out
          form
man listing
          next of kin
man told
          by travel folder
          that the people are hospitable
          and wear charming pantaloons
man reading
          another government depot blown up,
          only five civilians killed
man eying
          traffic more lunatic than Paris.

We can be sure that the latest warning
fired at Peking by *Izvestia*
did not go unnoticed in Washington.
The question is what is really being thought there.
They say he is willing to meet with his counterpart
          any time   any place
but he is not going to be the first man
in the White House to lose a war.

Addressing Congress last week,
                          he appeared
sad and tired,
             as if he had no alternative
now but to persist
                 and was still hearing
the man on the street,
                      dark, crossed daggers
in the eyes of the old coot,
                          "I'd give them 48
hours to come to the conference table."
                                 If they didn't come,
hardware would take over.
                      Uber alles, Age of Hardware.

Make no mistake about it, the Man of the Bomb
is not just your ordinary solid citizen
jerking off in his beer.
It could be anybody
                  with a grievance:
the smiling grocer
the farmer with a single plow
the muscular working
                   man
the old
      man in black
on social security
anybodies in a hurry
                  to get back to the Greenbay Packers.
That takes in a lot of territory,
especially when you consider
that government is power . . .
                          Hail!

and power has responsibility.
                                    Ah, that's the word
                                    that seals us in!
Thus, great nations are called Powers by the realists
                                    and lowers the coffin
                                    of the average citizen
and Great Powers have Great Enemies
                                    who is only dimly aware
                                    though drilled to be alert
as if to say, if power were a unicorn,
the others would be watching
                                    for the slightest deviation
from its public stance on unicorn.
A fraction of a millimeter,
                         and the game would be over,
the secret would be out: a paper unicorn!
Thus, Great Powers never yield,
for power can not endure humiliation.
                         Thus, the citizens
                         of Lower Slobbovia
                         will always have honor.
So it is writ about an orderly universe.
This is the tacit rule of governors,
the hub of nations,
                         the axletree of world-order
as undeniable and determinate   as the unicorn.

Events suggest that the administration
has been caught in a rat's bind
by its own rhetoric on commitments,
but the average citizen goes about his work
even when it's **his** son
                who's been sent home
in a simple box
            and left on the siding.
The underlying mood of the nation is steady and mild.
It shows a patience which allows the president
              maximum leeway.
Though the father says, "I can't hunt anymore.
I can't pick up a gun.
            It's that boy.
We used to hunt and fish together,"
he is careful to avoid complaining.

American technology is not so thoughtful.
Smallest in its showcase
is the little Cessna spotter plane.
Its function is to flush out Charlie.
Not the venerable Asian in the field below.
No, Charlie is not a thing or person.
It's a process   for converting man.
In three stages
          he becomes The Enemy,
the target,
        finally no-man
shortly to be splashed across his field,
shortly to be buried,
bleeding scraps of guts and gristle.
Charlie the hapless victim of superior know-how
with whom the American god carried on a chase
and shared a moment of intimacy,
              if not affection,
before he came apart in the range finder.

I am afraid the American god
does not take Charlie very seriously.

"All I got today were two water buffaloes
                  (approximately two years' income
                              for a farmer)
and a pregnant woman."
                  Hunter's world.
The hunter can afford to joke.
He has made the creatures
                  of Genesis his game.

Tell us again the object
in the range finder is not a man.

The object
in the range finder is not a man.
It's Charlie,
            never a child or woman
(the hunter is galant)
though regretfully in such an operation
the margin of error approaches infinity.

Tell us again, who is Charlie?
                  who is Charlie?

The nights are very long for the global American.
The winds are chill. Lincoln would have understood
these times. He prays
and likes to barbecue outdoors
and tear down back roads
                              at eighty miles an hour.
He has nothing against these people.
But they must learn that aggression can never win.
It has been necessary therefore to persevere
and call in the absolute:
                              firepower the god of ending.
Out rushes flaming napalm
                              with its white phosphorus fuse
along roads and river banks,
roaring into gunpits, tunnels, villages,
sucking the oxygen out of Charlie
as he cringes under his floorboards;
helicopters hosing down machine gun fire,
Huey Hogs, floating platforms firing batallion-strength,
thundering, jet-fast cluster bombs,
one looking like an exotic guava.

But most god of all, the real pros,
are the men of the B-52,
diffident, reliable young men
with steel-trap minds,
the exquisite defenders of their country,
already designated to deliver the Big One
                              if and when.

Less ultimate, more merciful,
their orders here are to reduce to ash
even the turtle dozing in the deep cave.
Mile by mile methodically the provinces
of Bin Dinh, Phu Yen, Pleiku, Quang Ngai,
                                                        by instrument
so fast
        it takes a moment
for the air to explode.

They sit in a honky-tonk
(some 14,000 whore houses in Saigon)
                                        motionless.
From time to time pick up a glass
from the table
                        slow, mechanical,
and take a drink.
Observe the thirteen year old whore—
                        so young, and so unkind a word—
whose virginity was sold for 15,000 piastres
to a rich old Cholonese
by an educated man about town
who became her customer.
Their bright young faces
are singularly handsome and untroubled.

They had mothers.
                    What has been done to them?

And to these gentle, patient men,
this ancient culture
                    in which women walk
as if measure were all,
                    and children could charm
a lizard out of a tree.

Peace,
          I dare not call you shepherd,
                              mother,
more complex than atomic science,
are you not native to our cities?
to our fears and angers?
Must you be brief? conditional?

So sweet,
          yet so uncertain!

XVII   A Reminder of William Carlos Williams

How quickly the dandelions
come up
      after a rain.
I picked them
         all
only yesterday.

XVIII   Atmosphere Anthrax

I would rather sing folk songs against injustice
and sound like ash cans in the early morning
or bark like a wolf
from the open doorway of a red-hot freight
than sit like Chopin on my exquisite ass.

XIX   **Item**

Why is a wizard
                    referred to with admiration
and a witch
              as foul?

Look into this,
              O women's liberation movement!

XX   The Sense of History

It is not the roll
                    your own
cigarette paper
                    that is gay
and open
            and unmistakably American
but the trade-mark

                    The Zigzag
Sailor.

XXI   Americana

lies in a glass
               and bronze
case

indecipherable
               sealed

in helium
            under the eyes

of a black
            guard
in the National Archives

and is lifted ineluctably
                   on electric jacks
from an underground tale.

Fiddling a Round

Go, imagination,
doodle,
        run amuck
while I am fiddling
desperately for a theme.
Distract me
            from my authentic self.
Show what you can do
with a lowly word like *fiddling*.

"I would rather hear
a roomful of aldermen
fiddling over a tavern license
than a writer fiddle on his grandiosity."

Bravo!

or "It's time you came, Orpheus,
to our steel tombs
and expelled all this intellectual fiddling."

I'll drink to that.

"Give me the fiddling in a fairy ring
                        of fern"

Lovely. Positive it!

"and a fortuity of fiddling"

Now that's a horse
            of another fiddle.

"There's an existence of fiddles
perched like birds on a high
                        power line"

A hit! a palpable!

"and isn't the grasshoper's fiddle akimbo?"

That could put me into stitches
if it had a thread.

Consider also
                "awake to viols
                but condemned to fiddle"

ah, the human condition!

or "the poor beggar doesn't have a fiddle
to his obvious."

Who does?

Now to the bass string:
"The country fiddles
                    while the emotion burns
and The Great Powers
                    convene"

Now **there** is fiddling!
a tale of vice versa,
the fiddling of a battle
                    of jaws,
or of instant history
as when the emperor of Rome cried, "Let her burn!"

and finally "Einstein's infinite
                    fiddle"

Ah, I could lay me down in such a featherbed
and travel to Alpha Centauri on an imaginary number.

"But where are the fiddles of Israel?"

Aleph the ox in Hebrew takes a grave measure.
Let us play it like we feel.

And where are the scribblings
                    of yesteryear?

fiddled away! fiddled away!

Short Story

Ah, toucan, we meet again!
Exactly as he looked ten years ago,
tall and slim as an Italian count,
the nose like that Bolivian bird.
Light and bouncy.
On his way to the same caper.

O for a quixotic tongue
to sparkle
          like this air!

If I were not related to the right people
would he greet me so extravagantly?
Maybe it's embarrassment,
the paper bag he's carrying?

Business failure.
                  But a chaser?
So they say.
          Strange tastes.
They must find him amorous.
Those ardent eyes
never leave theirs
till they yield.
Long and lovingly,
that's the ticket.
Too late then.
Might as well go on.
Just curious at first.
What is it like?
Those dark eyes
always urging,
imploring,
to bed!

Must be damned flattering.
Too much for them.
Out of reasons.
Tell themselves
deserve a change
                    of luck.

Every inch the count,
though afterwards they like to tease:
what happened to you
                    my little count?

And so he goes
                    under
those lacy frills
down down to woman,
held by that musk.

Open! Open!

Tonight your wife
will bed down
with your ectoplasm.

Hasta la vista,
                    toucan!
See you on the next round.

I'll be older.

Drinking Song

After Moses Ibn Ezra

Bring me that sickly looking wine glass.
See, when I fill it
it becomes as ardent as a lover's face
and chases off my beelzebubs.

Drink, my friend, and pass the beaker
So I may unburden myself
and if you see me going under
revive me with your minstrelsy.

Song

After Jehudah Halevi

Let the morning pursue me
with the wind that senses her body
and let the clouds carry my message.
Then might she yield.

Lying in the constellation of The Bear,
have pity, gazelle, on him who must fly
to the stars to reach you.

Song

After Jehudah Halevi

On the wind
in the cool of the evening
I send greetings to my friend.

I ask him only to remember the day
of our parting when we made a covenant
of love by an apple tree.

Song

After Moses Ibn Ezra

Circumstance has estranged my friend.
He has bolted the door
but I will enter the portal
and knock
         despite my enemies.
I will shatter locks with words.
I will break bolts with my songs
and will persuade myself
that nettles are sprigs of balsam.
I will dance and shout to their bitter juice
as if I were drunk on wine
and humble myself
and pretend that hell stream is icy
if it will get me through the darkness
                        into his light.

Go now, my song,
take this message to my beloved,
for song is a faithful messenger.

71

Young Couples Strolling By

When we get a good day here
                    the bee is at meridian
and little girls in worn-out slippers
charm the adversary
                    in the stranger's eye.

Incognito then enters
                    the coupling influence of the sun
licking an ice cream cone
and Swedes become Italians
                    and Italians become lizards
and Diogenes goes sailing.

Discoveries, Trade Names,
Genitals, and Ancient Instruments

If there is no connection between the wild
                           hemp of Kashmir
and the plectrum on a Persian lute,
                      the mind
will make one before the mallet comes down
                           on the cymbalo.
As the young people have discovered,
it can also make a Pax Americana
out of genitals and meditation.
So while it notes that Ghulan Quadir Zardar,
                      the Hasheesh King,
has been arrested in a taxi on his way to Srinagar,
let's steal a gay name from a love potion
and call ourselves HI-JOHN THE CONQUEROR ROOT.

Nature of Yellow

Topaz and dandelion,
                              yes,
and crow's foot
(that's an odd one)
and quince is
                    of the essence;
in a quince, in other words,
                                        like "in a nutshell";
but xanthite, icterus, ecru . . .
these are *yellow*?

The Romantic Eye

On the eight thousandth magnification
the chromosome of the Chironomus fly
stirred its microscopic nebulae
into the figure of a Greek Orthodox cross.

Comets in Triads

Atomic
          man
streamed

into
     cosmos
on

a
  mathematical
formula.

Poetic
          man
streamed

into
     destiny
on

a
  reading.
Silence!

Instantly
          the
mind

controlled
          the
question

by
  a
category

but
    intuito
the

maestro
          of
the

absolute
          and
signior

serio
    the heart
answered.

The Medium

I   The Oath

I lack Born's modesty
who was so touched by the magnitude of Einstein
that he could not work in that field.

I shall sit at his feet
though it is not my nature.

Sad, my course is laid out on the expedient.
Help me, tempest! Be my physician.

If my note is plain,
                    let it come out so.

The mad poet has been here
clowning and sounding alarums when he is pricked.
Let it be bound too
                    on the tail of its sperm
by oath and stipulation,

and condemn me to games
if I contaminate my true note.

I swear this by my nature.
Do not let me waver from it, physician.

II   **Parnassus**

A new breed overruns
                    from all
points of the compass,
the gray cats of mental operation.

Where are the old warriors
and the incorruptible humanists?

Where have I been?

III   How to Be Discovered As a Great Bard

Learn the grandiose manner
                        and the unending Orphic line.

Idolize a master
and attach yourself to one tit (one is plenty).

Represent the weakness of the age.

Keep at it for forty years
                     (preferably underground).

IV   **Sights**

I mean to penetrate the particular
the way an owl waits
                for a kangaroo rat
and the photomicrograph
beholds the hairy
                pappus of a dandelion.

V   **Stopping When You're Ahead**

My friend Robert Bly once named a poem,
After Drinking All Night with a Friend, We Go Out
in a Boat to See Who Can Write the Best Poem.

Being already in Cathay
                    I would have stopped right there.
Another word could only sink the boat
                              (it did).

Am I then lacking in enterprise?

So I am full of fun.

I could be satisfied to call a poem
                    The Assistant Person,
for example, and let anybody who can leap
to attention fill in the rest
but the academicians would not be able
to stand the uncertainty.

VI   The Owl As a Prose Model

His element is silent and inexorable.
Mack the Knife waits in his eyes.
Yet he is generous and brings his young
eleven mice, four bullheads,
thirteen grouse, two eels,
three rabbits and a woodcock,

                              all in one night.

One who is not capable of bungling
can afford to act low-keyed and imperturbable,
which always looks impersonal and clean.

This may be too much to expect of prose,
but is there any reason why
it could not be the scourge of rats
and learn from his exact

                    knowledge of his object?
of his eyes, claws, wings?
It might, like him, then live

                        to sixty-eight years
and look wise.

VII   **Ernest Hemingway**
             1899–1961

How imperceptibly the imagination
makes a manly ground
when it feels impotent.

At least I did not perpetrate
the infinitely expansible
Orphic phallusies
in fashion now.

VIII   **The Poet to His Reviewer**

It is customary to rave about poetry.
           Why don't you?

You tapped the champion
on the shoulder,
          country boy,
and broke his ankle.

Out crept my cowering mouse.
Beat it, you crummy beast,
before we're discovered!

IX   Letter to the Critic

There's no living with you
when you pass yourself off as an interpreter.
For whom is this game played?

Are you less entitled to imagination than the poet?
Django on a borrowed string,
I'll vote for that!

X   The Pastoral

The celebrated
                    artist whose wild lines
sell for seventy-five thousand dollars a canvas
is being interviewed:
                              In violence I saw pastoral.
Added
        who asked him?
the admiring critic:
The natural
                    act of the modern artist
one of the great
                          under
privileged classes
                        of history.

O turtle dove!
                    O superior intellect!

The Experiment with a Rat

Every time I nudge that spring
                        a bell rings
and a man walks out of a cage
assiduous and sharp like one of us
and brings me cheese.

                How did he fall
                        into my power?

Index of Titles

Index of First Lines

DATE DUE

DEMCO 38-297